THE LITTLE BOOK OF HOW TO SURVIVE

C000017692

AND BEYOND
by Richard Hession

Published in the UK by
LITTLE **BLACK**DOG LIMITED
Unit 3 Everdon Park
Heartlands Business Park
NN11 8YJ

Telephone   01327 871 777
Facsimile   01327 879 222
E Mail   info@littleblackdogltd.co.uk

Cover and interior layout by Sanjit Saha
Cover Design & Illustration Sanjit Saha

ISBN 9781904967743

Printed and bound in China by 1010 International

Never trust anyone over 30.

(Jerry Rubin)

This actress I knew, when I was 31, she was 36. When I got to 40, she was 37. That must have been some year!

(Tony Curtis)

Middle age is when work is a lot less fun,
and fun is a lot more work.

(Milton Berle)

We all deserve more years between 28 and 40

(James Thurber)

We are the people our mothers' warned
us against.

(John Lennon)

Teenagers are God's punishment for having sex.

(Steve Martin)

Children are great comforters in old age,
and they also help you to reach it faster.

(Lionel Kauffmann)

When a man of 30 falls in love with a girl of 20, it's not her youth he's seeking, but his own.

People ought to retire at 30 when they feel over-used and go back to work at 65 when they feel useless.

(Carol Anne O'Marie)

Thirty is that time in a man's life when his daydreams centre round a bank manager saying yes instead of a girl.

(Jane Fonda)

You know you've reached middle-age
when your weightlifting consists merely of
standing up.

(Bob Hope.)

Thirty is the age when you stop patting yourself on the head and start under the chin.

Women over 40 are at their best, but men over 30 are too old to recognise it.

(Jean Paul Belmondo.)

The great comfort of turning 30 is the
realisation that you are now too old to
die young.

(Paul Dickson)

Thirty is when everything new you feel is likely to be a symptom.

Do what you have to do to be happy in this life.

(*Bridges of Maddison County*)

It's pretty hard to tell what does bring happiness, poverty and wealth have both failed.

He whoever said money does not buy happiness does not know where to shop.

Never make someone else the source of your happiness.

The nice thing about being happy at 30 is that you never think you will be unhappy again.

When friends ask for criticism, they usually want praise.

Friends are God's compensation for relatives.

Make it simple, keep it easy

A wise man knows everything,
a shrewd man knows everyone

Confess yesterday's folly
as it bestows wisdom today.

It is better to be hated for whom you are,
than loved for whom you are not

Never turn a quarrel into a feud

Aim for the pools of possibility, avoiding
the puddles of problems on the way

I won't be wronged or insulted or laid a hand on, I don't do this to others, I won't have them do it to me

The real voyage of discovery consists not in seeking new landscapes, but in having new eyes.

(Proust)

He who desires the pearl must dive deep.

Life is ours to be spent, not saved.

(D.H. Lawrence.)

Past performance is not necessarily a guide to the future.

(Norwich Union.)

When you live in a world of doom and gloom, it's hard to be warm and rosy.

(Felix Severn)

Mediocracy is self-inflicted, genius is self bestowed.

Anything you try and fix will cost more
and takes longer than you thought.

We should learn from our mistakes but really study our successes.

When opportunity knocks, open the door,
if not its knuckles get sore and it moves
on.

He who hesitates usually survives, but
when you snooze you lose!

The best thing about the truth is that you don't have to remember what you said.

Good Advice - "Retire before you become famous".

(George Harrison.)

I always say what I think,
but am careful to whom I say it.

(Felix Severn)

Bite off more than you can chew and chew like buggery.

(*Paul Hogan.*)

Be slow to make a promise
but quick to keep it.

Beauty is only skin deep,
ugly goes to the bone.

The difference between genius and madness is the degree of success.

There is no justice,
just us.

Seek first to understand, then be understood.

Choose between life on the edge or
retirement on the horizon

Second thoughts are best

Face your fears and live your dreams,

('T' shirt logo)

Nothing is out of reach with resourcefulness

A handful of good life is
better than a ton of learning

For they who has nothing,
everything awaits

It's always easier to decide you cannot
do something than decide you can

Of all the things you wear, your expression is the most important

Don't think of yesterday, don't worry about tomorrow, focus on today

The only place where Success comes
before Work is in the dictionary.

(Vidal Sassoon)

Discovery consists of seeing what everyone has seen and thinking what no-one has thought.

Crank - a man with a new idea until it succeeds.

(Mark Twain)

Life is what happens while you're busy
making other plans.

(John Lennon)

A good plan today is better than a great
plan tomorrow

Avoid dying in debt
and being owed in life

If the quest is right
never give up

Better to be at the bottom of a ladder you want to climb than halfway up one you don't.

(The Office)

An ounce of imagination is worth a pound of facts

Never do anything to jeopardise
your own efforts.

(X-Files)

Imagination is more important
than knowledge.

(*Albert Einstein.*)

You have two ears and one mouth - use them in proportion.

(Patrick Hession)

The best things in life aren't things.

Artificial intelligence is no match for natural stupidity.

Never underestimate the power of very stupid people in large groups.

A closed mouth gathers no feet.

If you don't know where you are going,
all roads lead there.

(The Cheshire Cat.)

Persuading me I am stupid is not a good way to win the argument.

If you stay calm when all around is chaos, you have probably failed to understand the situation.

Everyone has a scheme for getting rich
that won't work.

Indecision is the key to flexibility.

To talk without thinking is
to shoot without aiming.

Experience is the name so many people give to their mistakes.

(Oscar Wilde.)

The fool regrets what has been said, the wise man considers what has to be said.

Asking a stupid question is better than correcting a stupid mistake.

Some are wise and some are otherwise.

If you don't stand for something,
you will fall for anything.

Everyone makes mistakes
only fools persist in them.

Practice does not make perfect,
only permanent.

Nobody loves a fat man
except his grocer.

Love is like a teabag
only in hot water do
you see it's strength.

Freedom is as free as your opponent is.

(Vera Luxamburg)

Forgive your enemies,
but never forget their names.

(JFK)

Winners never quit and quitters never win.

(Richard Nixon.)

I don't make mistakes,
I learn from the mistakes of others.

(O. Bismark.)

You can order other Little books directly from Little Black Dog. All at relevant retail prices each including postage (UK only)

Postage and packing outside the UK: Europe: add 20% of retail price Rest of the world: add 30% of retail price

To order any book please call 01327 871 777

LITTLE **BLACK**DOG LIMITED 3 Everdon Park, Heartlands Business Park, Daventry NN11 8YJ